Read[...]spond

Talk about it

Get writing

Assessment

Author: Celia Warren

Development Editor: Simret Brar

Editor: Sarah Sodhi

Assistant Editor: Pam Kelt

Series Designer: Anna Oliwa

Designed by: Macmillan Publishing Solutions

Illustrator: Axel Scheffler

Designed using Adobe InDesign

Published by Scholastic Ltd, Villiers House,
Clarendon Avenue, Leamington Spa,
Warwickshire CV32 5PR

www.scholastic.co.uk

Printed by Bell & Bain

1 2 3 4 5 6 7 8 9 9 0 1 2 3 4 5 6 7

British Library Cataloguing-in-Publication Data
A catalogue record for this book is available from the British Library.

ISBN 978-1407-10213-9

Acknowledgements

The publishers would like to thank **Scholastic UK** for the use of text and illustrations from *Tiddler* by Julia Donaldson, text © 2007, Julia Donaldson, illustrations © 2007, Axel Scheffler (2007, Alison Green Books). Every effort has been made to trace copyright holders for the works reproduced in this book, and the publishers apologise for any inadvertent omissions.

Tiddler

SECTION 1

About the book

Well-known children's author Julia Donaldson has teamed up with illustrator Axel Scheffler for this delightful picture book. It tells the tale of Tiddler, a tiny fish in a big ocean, who has a great adventure. The book itself is a celebration of storytelling and the imagination, and demonstrates how stories (and, by implication, jokes and fairy tales) are invented and then spread from person to person. It reminds us how much we all love to hear and tell stories.

Told in rhyming verse, with an attractively addictive rhythm, its strong beat and repetitive phrases beg children to join in and learn sections by heart before they realise it. Its undersea setting has great appeal, as do the genuine but amusing names of the fish, such as the teacher Miss Skate and Tiddler's classmates Spiderfish and Rabbitfish.

The story offers wide cross-curricular opportunities, from the study of ocean life and deep-sea habitats, to learning o'clock times, Roman numerals and days of the week. It also offers the opportunity to teach personal care and safety, such as the importance of going straight to school.

The clear, bright illustrations offer much scope for discussion and inferential comprehension. Treasure chests sit vividly on the seabed with no mention of how they arrived there, while mermaids add a further element of fantasy, neatly complementing discussion about the difference between truth and invention, which is central to the 'storytelling' theme of this book.

About the author

Julia Donaldson was born in 1948. She grew up in London but now lives in Glasgow with her husband Malcolm, whom she met when she was studying drama and French at Bristol University. She writes children's stories, rhyming stories for picture books, plays, poems and songs. It was when one of her songs, *A Squash and a Squeeze,* was produced as a book that she turned her hand to writing picture books and older fiction.

About the illustrator

Axel Scheffler was born in 1957 in Germany. He grew up in Hamburg, and came to the UK to study illustration. After graduating in Bath, he moved to London, where he continues to live with his family. Axel has illustrated dozens of successful children's books. His many picture books include ten written by Julia Donaldson. He has also created black-and-white line drawings for a wide range of older fiction.

Facts and figures

Tiddler has sold more than 110,000 copies. while the books of Julia Donaldson and Axel Scheffler have been translated into 30 languages, including Icelandic, Turkish, Korean, Chinese and Japanese. Other books by Julia Donaldson and Axel Scheffler include: *Room on the Broom; The Snail and the Whale; Monkey Puzzle; The Gruffalo; The Gruffalo's Child; The Smartest Giant in Town;* and *The Stick Man.*

Cover, title page and spread 1

Look at the pictures together and discuss the deep-sea setting of the story. Encourage the children to name some of the species they recognise, such as the seaweed, anemone, coral, colourful tropical fish (indicating it is a warm sea), octopus, walrus, jellyfish, lobster, shark, seahorse, crab and cuttlefish. Ask the children if they know what the collective noun for fish is. Explain that it is called a 'shoal'. Discuss how a treasure chest and unattached anchor might find their way to the seabed.

Ask the children to identify Tiddler from the description. Point out the words: 'plain grey scales'. Can they see the scales and the fins? Discuss the meaning of 'telling tales'. Explain that literally it means telling stories, but metaphorically it means telling lies or stretching the truth.

Invite the children to spot adjectives in the text, such as 'plain', 'grey', 'big', 'small' and 'tall', and verbs, such as 'riding', 'flying' and 'diving'. Point out how words beginning with the same sound (alliteration) add to the rhythm and rhyme of the verse structure of the story. Can the children identify the rhyming words? Can the children pick out the phrase Tiddler always uses when making his excuses for being late. Point out the words: "Sorry I'm late".

Spreads 2 and 3

Tell the children that all the characters' names are the names of real fish. Explain that they begin with capital letters in the story because they are also names. For example, there is a fish called a skate, whose name is used for the teacher, Miss Skate. Discuss how each fish is identifiable by its pattern, such as the spot on Johnny Dory's side and Rabbitfish's black and white head and yellow rear. Invite the children to describe each fish.

Read the page beginning 'At nine o'clock on Monday', inviting the children to answer the register in the roles of Rabbitfish and Redfin. Demonstrate a change of tone between the two callings of "Tiddler?". Invite the children to suggest why 'TIDDLER'S LATE!' is in capital letters. How do they think Miss Skate says this? How does she feel about Tiddler being late? She might be cross, exasperated or annoyed. Ask the children what the fish are learning about that day. Point out that they are drawing fishbone skeletons on their slates.

Ask the children who they think is speaking in the phrase: "Sorry I'm late." (Tiddler). Discuss the possibilities of who says "Oh, no, she didn't." and "OH, YES, SHE DID." Is it Miss Skate, or the other fish, or both? Or could it be Tiddler or Johnny Dory? There is no right or wrong answer. Point out that the speech marks open and close, indicating a change of speaker. Draw the children's attention to the way the reader can work out who is speaking in some cases, but in others the word 'said' is used.

Spreads 4 and 5

Discuss the similarities between this part of the story and the last two spreads. Point out that it is the same time of day and Miss Skate is calling the register. The names called are different and it is a new day, but the words 'TIDDLER'S LATE!' are repeated. Invite the children to compare Tiddler's excuse to his previous excuses. Can the children see it is more imaginative and exciting as Tiddler was apparently in danger this time?

Can the children spot the clues that suggest that Tiddler's excuses are made up? Highlight the fact that Tiddler's friends never believe him and that mermaids do not exist. Ask who likes Tiddler's tall stories best. Who does Little Johnny Dory tell the stories to? How do other fish get to hear the story?

Encourage the children to identify the rhymes and to join in the repeated phrases, especially the pantomime style, "OH, YES, HE DID." Before turning the page, can the children predict the time and day of the week that will begin the next part of the story?

Spreads 6 and 7

Ask the children if they know what 'dawdling' means. Which phrase tells us that Tiddler is using his 'big imagination' as he dawdles? Point out the words: 'Dreaming up a story, his tallest story yet'. Which phrase tells us that Tiddler was not concentrating and watching where he was going? Point out the words: 'Lost inside his story, he didn't see the fishing boat'.

Ask the children if they can guess what story Tiddler was dreaming up. Encourage the children to look at the illustration showing Tiddler stuck inside a green bottle, with penguins attempting to release him.

Before turning the page, invite the children to suggest what will happen next. Point out that the next line of the story will end with a word that rhymes with 'yet'.

Do the children notice that the word 'NET' is not only in capital letters, but also in a larger font? How does this reflect the horror of the story? Explain that this time it is not Tiddler's imagination, but a real, dangerous situation; the large, capital letters help to illustrate the drama.

Can the children guess what time of day it is? Explain that the word 'meanwhile' shows that these events are happening at the same time that Miss Skate is calling the register.

Discuss why Tiddler appears happy when he enters the fishermen's net. Does he realise what is happening? Encourage the children to describe how Tiddler will feel when he opens his eyes. Can the children recognise the irony of the words "TIDDLER'S LATE!"?

Spread 8

Ask the children who is watching the clock and missing Tiddler the most. Point out that the numbers on the clock are Roman numerals. Write the numbers 1 to 12 in Arabic numerals. Underneath write the Roman equivalents.

Ask the children to work out how late Tiddler is by 12 o'clock. Can they tell what the fish are having for lunch? How does the illustrator reinforce the sadness of Tiddler's situation when the fishermen haul in the fishing net? The children may not use the term 'pathetic fallacy', but they may notice how hard it is raining.

Ask the children what 'hauling' means. What does it suggest about the fishermen's load? Does it look heavy? Discuss why the pilot of the shipping boat looks more cheerful than the fishermen. Could it be because he is dry and under cover? Discuss why the gulls might be gathering around the boat.

Spreads 9 and 10

Ask the children how Tiddler differs from the fish that are not thrown back to sea. Do they notice that he is smaller? Draw their attention to the word 'ocean', which is synonymous with 'sea'. Tiddler is lost in unfamiliar waters. Discuss how he might be feeling.

Where do the 'strange lights' that glimmer come from? Tell the children about neon fish that glow in the dark depths of the sea, and angler fish which have a light 'lure'. Compare the word 'glimmered' to 'glowed' and 'shimmered'. Ask the children if fish really can fly. Explain that there are several species of so-called 'flying fish', whose large fins enable them to glide through the air. Can the children say what the ellipsis at the end of spread ten tells the reader?

Explain that it shows the sentence continues on the next page, and that a significant event is about to happen.

Spreads 11 and 12

Ask the children which word of the story Tiddler hears is most likely to attract his attention. Do they guess it is his name? Point to his name as you read the story, waiting for the children to say it at the beginning of each sentence.

Discuss how Tiddler would feel on hearing his own story being retold. Can the children spot Tiddler in the shoal of anchovies as they take him to meet the shrimp? Encourage them to explain how he is recognisable using comparative words, such as 'bigger' and 'fatter'.

Invite the children to notice that each creature named as the storyteller is the next one that Tiddler visits in his attempt to find his way home. For example, the whale says "I heard it from a herring", so Tiddler approaches the herring, who says he "heard it from an eel", so Tiddler visits the eel, and so on.

Spreads 13

Encourage the children to look at the o'clock times and work out how long the fish have been at school. Can the children spot how some of the fish are fooling around? (One fish is flicking sand over his neighbour; another is nibbling his friend's tail.) Which fish is alone? (Little Johnny Dory.) Why is he looking miserable? (He is missing Tiddler.) Compare Johnny Dory with Granny Dory. How can they tell they are related? (Distinctive matching markings and shape.)

Spreads 14 and 15

Ask the children what emotion they think the large capital letters indicate in the following: 'IN SWAM TIDDLER at half past three!'. Can they tell you who believes Tiddler? Do the children make a link between the author and the 'writer friend'?

Shared reading

SECTION 3

Extract 1

- These are the opening lines of the book and the text layout shows the traditional verse form. Underline end-of-line rhymes: 'scales' and 'tales'; 'ray' and 'day'.
- Discuss the meaning of 'wasn't much to look at' with the children.
- Encourage the children to read the words with you as you point to them, until they achieve the intended rhythm.
- Underline adjectives in the first section ('plain', 'grey', 'big') and verbs in the second section ('riding', 'flying', 'diving', 'told').
- Highlight the opening and closing speech marks. Explain that, because it is Tiddler speaking each time, the newly opened speech marks show the excuse belongs to a new day.
- Examine how the repeated phrase reinforces the fact that Tiddler is always late.

Extract 2

- Compare Tiddler's excuse in the first section with those from Extract 1. Encourage the children to notice how Tiddler is expanding on his simple excuses, embroidering them with extra detail. Again, highlight the speech marks to show how they close and reopen with each fresh speaker.
- Underline the capital letters and explain that they are used for volume and to show emotion. Do the children spot the second change of font (the italics)? Invite their suggestions as to what purpose they serve. Challenge individuals to read from the extract, varying their tone, pace and volume as appropriate.
- Underline rhymes, both at ends of lines ('lid', 'DID'; 'Dab', 'crab') and within lines ('bashed', 'thrashed'). Discuss how the rhyme enhances the image of the small fish trying to escape.
- Discuss why the subject and verb are missing from Dragonfish and Dab's speech: "[It's] Just a silly story". Explain that it follows on from Rabbitfish and Redfin's speech, which is a more natural, colloquial way of speaking.
- Re-read the passage, inviting individual children to read the direct speech and the whole group to read "OH, YES, SHE DID." Encourage the children to observe where speech marks open and close.

Extract 3

- Highlight the apostrophes and discuss that the following letters or words are missing: 'nine o[f the] clock'; 'did n[o]t'; "TIDDLER [I]S LATE".
- Underline the use of initial capital letters for days of the week, names and titles, new lines of verse and new sentences. Reinforce the use of capital letters for giving emphasis, volume and impact ("TIDDLER'S LATE!").
- Draw a dividing line between the two halves of compound words to show their component parts (fisher/men; mean/while; school/room; Leopard/fish).
- Highlight the ellipsis (...) and discuss its purpose of indicating that something important or exciting is to follow.
- Ring each verb, comparing the '-ing' ending of the present participle, for example, 'dawdling', 'dreaming', the root verbs that follow 'didn't' ('see', 'hear', 'spot') and the '-ed' of the past tense ('called').

Extract 1

Once there was a fish and his name was Tiddler.
He wasn't much to look at, with his plain grey scales.
But Tiddler was a fish with a big imagination.
He blew small bubbles but he told tall tales.

"Sorry I'm late. I was riding on a seahorse."

"Sorry I'm late. I was flying with a ray."

"Sorry I'm late. I was diving with a dolphin."

Tiddler told a different story every day.

Extract 2

"Sorry I'm late. I was swimming round a shipwreck.
I swam into a treasure chest, and someone closed the lid.
I bashed and I thrashed till a mermaid let me out again."
"Oh, no, she didn't." "OH, YES, SHE DID."

"It's only a story," said Rabbitfish and Redfin.

"Just a silly story," said Dragonfish and Dab.

"I *like* Tiddler's story," said Little Johnny Dory,

And he told it to his granny, who told it to a crab.

Extract 3

At nine o'clock on Wednesday,
Tiddler was dawdling,
Dreaming up a story,
his tallest story yet.

Lost inside his story,
he didn't see the fishing boat.

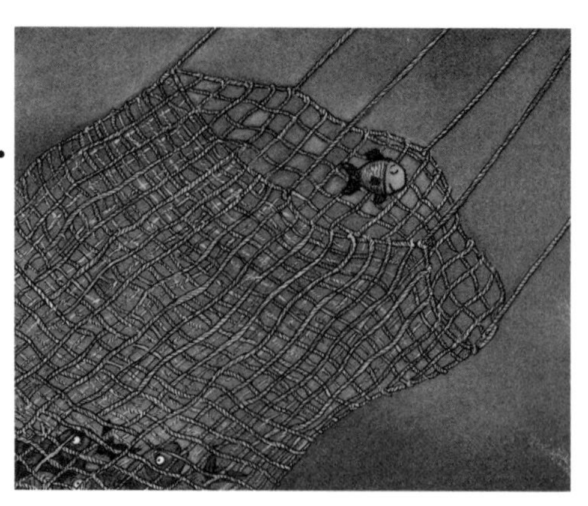

He didn't hear the fishermen.
He didn't spot...

... the NET.

Meanwhile, in the schoolroom,
Miss Skate called the register.
"Little Johnny Dory?"

"Yes, Miss Skate."

"Leopardfish?" "Yes, Miss."

"Leaf Fish?" "Yes, Miss."

"Tiddler? Tiddler?

TIDDLER'S LATE!"

Meeting Tiddler

Objective: To listen with enjoyment to a story, sustain attentive listening, responding to what the children have heard with relevant comments questions or actions.
You will need: Teacher copy of *Tiddler,* quiet, comfortable story area.
Cross-curricular link: Natural science.

What to do

- Talk about where the children might see living fish, such as in rivers, lakes, fish tanks, pools and the sea.
- Show them the cover of *Tiddler* and discuss the setting of the story. Discuss which things, other than the fish, help to identify the setting, such as the walrus, anemones and treasure chest.
- Read the title, moving your finger left to right along the words. Ask: *Is Tiddler likely to be a big or small fish? Why does his name suit him?* Note the word 'tiddler' without a capital letter.
- Explain that Tiddler goes to school with other fish. Their teacher also has a fishy name. As she calls the register, each fish replies "Yes, Miss".
- Read the story out loud, emphasising the rhythm and rhymes. Let the children join in the repetitive phrases.
- Did the children spot the author in the book? Can they explain why she is in a diving suit? Ask: *What happened to the story after she had written it down?*

Differentiation
For older/more confident learners: Create a list of Tiddler's friends' names for the children to copy and recreate Miss Skate's register. Re-read the story, asking them to tick each name as they hear it.
For younger/less confident learners: Discuss the pictures in the book. Ask: *What are the fish drawing on their slates? How did the turtle rescue Tiddler? What do the fish eat at lunchtime?*

Tiddler's factfile

Objective: To identify the main character in a story, and find specific information in simple texts.
You will need: Copies of *Tiddler,* enlarged copy of Extract 1 on photocopiable page 8, photocopiable page 15, writing materials, shades of grey crayons.

What to do

- After the children have listened to the story, display Extract 1 from photocopiable page 8.
- Point out that these eight lines provide all the characteristics of the main character. Read them together with the children, as you point to the text.
- List the aspects of Tiddler's character that are shown: name, appearance, habits and behaviour. Point out that the direct speech helps the reader to 'hear' Tiddler's voice.
- Explain the value of adjectives when describing a character. When the children identify them, underline them ('plain', 'grey', 'big', 'small', 'tall').
- Ask individuals to read the lines that tell us:
  - who the character is (line one)
  - what his talent is (lines three and four)
  - what he looks like (line two)
  - what he does regularly (line eight).
- Invite the whole group to call out Tiddler's catchphrase ("Sorry I'm late").
- Hand out copies of the photocopiable sheet and encourage the children to use the story to complete Tiddler's factfile.

Differentiation
For older/more confident learners: Ask the children to add a second speech bubble and write their favourite excuse in it, using the book for reference.
For younger/less confident learners: Write the missing adjectives in the spaces. Invite the children to cut out and match the correct words from the foot of the page.

Picture the scene

Objective: To recognise the main elements that shape different texts.
You will need: Copies of *Tiddler*, photocopiable page 16 enlarged for each child, writing materials.
Cross-curricular link: Art.

What to do

- After the children have listened to the story, retell it in a prose style. Ask: *Is this the same story? How does the retelling differ?* Point out that it does not use rhyme, rhythm or other poetic devices.
- Re-read the opening lines from the book, focusing on the rhythm and pausing for the children to supply the rhymes.
- Explain that without the pictures the text is a story poem. The pictures tell the story as much as words.
- Point out that sometimes the words tell the illustrator what to draw ('plain grey scales'). At other times he follows clues to picture the scene.
- Without showing the picture, read: "I swam into a treasure chest, and someone closed the lid." Ask: *Does the author say who? Can we guess? Can we get any ideas from the picture?*
- Hand out copies of *Tiddler* along with the photocopiable page. Ask the children to find each quotation and study the pictures to answer each question.

Differentiation
For older/more confident learners: Challenge the children to describe or draw alternative interpretations of one of the quotations. For example, "a turtle came and rescued me" might show the turtle knotting the squid's tentacles.
For younger/less confident learners: Cut out each quotation for the children to match the words with the original text. Ask the children to discuss alternative suggestions in small groups.

Again and again

Objective: To explore the effect of patterns of language and repeated words and phrases.
You will need: Copies of *Tiddler,* books of traditional stories and nursery rhymes, whiteboard or flipchart, writing materials.

What to do

- Compare the way you call the register to Miss Skate in *Tiddler*. Point out the pattern where the teacher and the children take turns to speak.
- Can the children suggest other phrases that are regularly repeated, such as 'Pencils down!', 'Please may I be excused?' and 'Well done!'?
- Divide the class into groups of five and look through the book for all the repeated phrases.
- Hold the book so the children can see the pictures and re-read the story, stopping for the children to call out the repeated phrases.
- Ask the children if there is repetition in the setting, plot and characters. Point out that both the language and plot follow a repetitive pattern of phrase, rhyme and metre.
- Tell the class they are going to play a game called Chinese whispers. Invite the child sitting on your left to make up a sentence and whisper it to the child next to them, who then passes it on until the words have gone round the class. The last child tells everyone what they heard. Ask: *How much has the sentence changed?*

Differentiation
For older/more confident learners: Challenge the children to find other stories that contain repeated phrases, such as "I'll huff and I'll puff and I'll blow your house down" and "All the better to [see] you with".
For younger/less confident learners: Encourage the children to recite nursery rhymes that include repetitive patterns, such as 'This Little Piggy Went to Market' and 'Polly Put the Kettle On'.

A recommended read?

Objective: To explain their reactions to texts, commenting on important aspects.
You will need: Copies of *Tiddler,* enlarged copies of photocopiable page 17, writing materials.

What to do

- When the children are familiar with the book, ask them if they enjoyed the story. Ask: *Do you want to read it again? Did you like the characters and setting? Can you recite any parts by heart? Does it have a satisfying ending? Is it a book you would enjoy reading to younger siblings? Why?*
- Discuss the children's responses. Point out that a show of hands is a quick way to find out how many children agree.
- Explain that there are different ways to choose a book: flick through the pages, read a couple of pages, look at the pictures, read the back-cover blurb, choose a favourite author/illustrator or read reviews.
- Hand out the photocopiable sheet and explain that they are going to write about *Tiddler,* telling readers a little about the plot, main character and setting, and explaining if and why they would recommend it to others to read.

Differentiation
For older/more confident learners: Ask the children to add a section: 'Books by the same author'. Encourage them to use the library or internet to research information.
For younger/less confident learners: Act as scribe, asking the children questions to prompt their discussion, helping to turn their answers into complete sentences.

Fishy facts

Objective: To distinguish fiction and non-fiction texts and the different purposes for reading them.
You will need: Copies of *Tiddler,* photocopiable page 18, Extract 2 on photocopiable page 9, writing materials.
Cross-curricular link: Natural science.

What to do

- Display Extract 2 and the photocopiable sheet so the children cannot read the words. Ask: *Can you tell which is fiction and which is non-fiction?* Talk about the text layout, capital letters, speech marks and sub-titles.
- Bring the texts closer towards the class and ask if the children can spot which words are common to both texts.
- Ask: *Do the names appear in the same order in the extract as in the information text? Why not?*
- Compare the styles of the two texts, reading sections aloud to hear the difference in 'voice'. Ask: *Which text would be helpful to identify fish? Which makes a better bedtime story?* Discuss why.
- Invite the children to list the names of fish from the story and not included on the factsheet. Together, work out where to position them in alphabetical order.
- Discuss how this type of organisation helps us to find information.

Differentiation
For older/more confident learners: Challenge the children to find out some facts about fish not included on the factsheet. Can they find names of other tropical fish?
For younger/less confident learners: Write the names of all the fish species they have found on cards for the children to sort alphabetically.

Treasure hunt

Objective: To use syntax and context when reading for meaning.
You will need: Copies of *Tiddler,* writing materials.

What to do

- Invite the children to look at spread 11, beginning ' "Tiddler rode a seahorse." '
- Point out that the second word in each of the first five lines ('rode', 'met', 'found') is a verb, following Tiddler's name and describing what he is doing. Explain that every full sentence has to have one.
- Can the children spot the verbs on the facing page? Compare 'looked' to the more descriptive 'peeped'. Encourage the children to *look* at you and then to *peep* at you from behind their hands.
- Suggest that descriptive verbs are valuable – worth their weight in gold. Let the children imagine they are going to swim through the book like Tiddler, digging for treasure. Allow them a few minutes to write down any valuable verbs they find.
- Give the children clues, such as definitions or synonyms, to identify the meanings of 'dawdling', 'captured', 'hauling', 'glimmered' and 'shivered'. Highlight any spelling points, such as the '-ed' past participle.
- Discuss how using exciting verbs builds up atmosphere, bringing a story to life.

Differentiation

For older/more confident learners: Ask the children to reuse their valuable verbs in their own sentences and in fresh contexts that help to reveal their meaning. Challenge them to learn how to spell these words.
For younger/less confident learners: Pair diffident readers with more confident readers, or have an adult help a small group to identify the verbs and act as scribe.

What next?

Objective: To make predictions showing an understanding of ideas, events and characters.
You will need: Copies of *Tiddler,* enlarged copy of Extract 3 on photocopiable page 10, whiteboard or flipchart, writing materials.

What to do

- Display the extract and read it together. The story ends on Wednesday. Ask: *What do you imagine might happen on Thursday? Will Tiddler will be late again?* Look at different possibilities, and ask the children to justify their opinions based on their knowledge of Tiddler. Ask: *Do people change? If so, is it likely to be temporary or permanent? Might Tiddler enjoy the celebrity and want to look for more adventures?*
- Together, using the extract as a model, decide how a 'next page' would begin. Write: 'At nine o'clock on Thursday, Tiddler was early.' Let the children suggest an antonym to 'dawdling' that retains the rhythm, such as 'hurrying'. Explain that Tiddler will not need an excuse and work towards a second line, such as, 'Tiddler wasn't dreaming, he was first in the queue.'
- Collect and list words that rhyme with 'queue'. Highlight any that might be useful to describe Tiddler's arrival. Let the children suggest what happens and help rephrase their suggestions to end with a rhyme.

Differentiation

For older/more confident learners: Challenge the children to rewrite the registration scene, with a different ending that rhymes with 'Skate'.
For younger/less confident learners: Ask children to work in pairs to work out alternative endings to the story to share with the class.

Tiddler's factfile

Use the words from the box to fill in the gaps.

Tiddler had ______________ ______________ scales.

Tiddler had a ______________ imagination.

Tiddler blew ______________ bubbles.

Tiddler told ______________ tales.

small plain tall big grey

Write Tiddler's favourite phrase in the speech bubble.

Picture the scene

Find these lines in *Tiddler*. Look at the pictures and answer the questions. The first is started for you.

1. I swam into a treasure chest, and someone closed the lid. Who?

It might have been ______________________________

____

2. I wriggled and I struggled till a turtle came and rescued me. How?

____

____

3. Dreaming up a story, his tallest story yet. What?

____

____

4. He swam around in circles. Why?

____

____

5. He told it to a writer friend. Where?

____

____

A recommended read?

Write about *Tiddler* and why you would recommend it to others to read.

About the book

Describe the setting, main character and what happens.

____

____

____

The presentation

Describe the style of writing, what it is like to read and the illustrations.

____

____

____

Would you recommend this book?

Who you would recommend this book to and why?

____

____

____

My favourite part is...

Explain why and give a quote from the book.

____

____

____

Fishy facts

Find these fish in *Tiddler.*

Cut them out and put them in alphabetical order.

Little Johnny Dory A deep-bodied fish with striking markings that include a dark blotch on its sides. It is found in warm, shallow waters. It has two dorsal fins, the front one being spiny.	**Sunfish** A strange-looking, deep-bodied fish with large fins, but no tail. A poor swimmer, it is carried along by the ocean currents.
Redfin A member of the perch family, this fish has six tapering bands of black around its body, with a blotch on its side to the rear of the first of its two dorsal fins. It has a humped back behind its head.	**Dragonfish** A deep-swimming fish, reaching depths of 1500m. It has a long barbel on its chin and sharp fang-like teeth.
Dab A mid-brown fish, found mainly in shallow areas with a sandy seabed. A slim species with hard scales.	**Rabbitfish** A slow-moving, sandy coloured fish with large, dark eyes. It stays close to the seabed and helps to keep the coral reefs clean by eating the algae.

Rhythmic register

Objective: To interpret a text by reading aloud with some variety of pace and emphasis.
You will need: Extract 3 on photocopiable page 10.
Cross-curricular links: Drama; Speaking and listening.

What to do

- Read aloud the second part of this extract beginning, 'Meanwhile, in the schoolroom'. Use your voice to demonstrate the different voices, rhythm and changing pace.
- Divide the children into groups of five and let each member play the role of the narrator, one of the three fish or the teacher, Miss Skate. Encourage each child to retain the rhythm as they swap between speakers.
- Come together and listen to each group recite their extract. Challenge the children to use names from their class instead.
- Clap the rhythm of 'Lit-tle John-ny Dor-y', counting the syllables. Invite the children to suggest names that match the rhythms of all the various fish.
- Work as a whole group to extend the register while retaining the syllable pattern. For example: "Little Molly Unwin?", "Yes, Miss Skate"; "Christopher", "Yes, Miss"; "Annabel? Annabel? Annabel's late!".
- Let the children stand in order as a reminder for their turn to speak. Narrate the introduction and try and retain the rhythm as you move through the 'register'.

Differentiation
For older/more confident learners: Challenge the children to write their own interpretation of the scene as a short play script.
For younger/less confident learners: Provide the children with two- and three-syllable names on cards sort into a suitable order with "Yes, Miss" cards. Have an adult act as narrator and prompt.

Would you credit it?

Objective: To retell stories, ordering events using story language.
You will need: Copies of *Tiddler.*
Cross-curricular links: Drama.

What to do

- Look at Tiddler's excuses for being late. Do the children notice that the first three are fairly simple and plausible in the setting?
- Invite the children to make up their own excuses for being late. Explain that the best tall stories begin with an element of truth before they expand into fantasy.
- Ask children to compare Tiddler's early excuses with the later ones. Do they notice them become longer, more detailed and less plausible?
- Let the children take turns to invent excuses in pairs. They should start off with something that is simple and plausible, but become more wildly inventive, detailed and harder to believe.
- Bring the children together to share the most incredible story. Praise their use of plausible elements and details that add interest and credibility.
- Ask the children which stories they liked best. What makes it memorable? Vote for the story most likely to appeal to Granny Dory.

Differentiation
For older/more confident learners: Encourage the children to develop their wildest excuse into a short piece of drama, acting it out and developing the atmosphere of their tale using increasingly expressive adjectives and verbs
For younger/less confident learners: Encourage the children to develop their ideas by asking questions and offering gentle prompts. Ask: *Did you peep over next-door's hedge on your way to school? What did you see that took you by surprise?*

Talk about it

SECTION 5

Missing!

Objective: To take turns to speak, listen to others' suggestions and talk about what they are going to do.
You will need: Copies of *Tiddler,* enlarged copies of photocopiable page 22, writing and colouring materials.
Cross-curricular link: Art.

What to do

- Ask the children to imagine what might have happened if Tiddler had not turned up when he did.
- Sort the children into groups of five to create an eye-catching 'missing' poster to find Tiddler. Encourage them to decide what information must appear. For example, name, school, description, who saw him last and when.
- Appoint a leader to each group, to ensure that everyone has a fair say, and a scribe, to make notes of the suggestions.
- Remind the children to look at the book for inspiration. For example, what was Tiddler doing just before the net caught him? Perhaps a gull spotted him. Maybe a starfish saw a fishing boat nearby. What time did he go missing? Tell the children to imagine they are reading the poster. Is there any extra information they could add?
- Let each group have a photocopiable sheet to create their poster. Remind them to use colour effectively.

Differentiation
For older/more confident learners: Encourage the children to mount their poster on to card to add definition or to transfer their ideas on to an appropriate computer program and print a copy.
For younger/less confident learners: Help the children to draft their wording ready to copy it on to the photocopiable page.

The person I most admire

Objective: To tell stories and describe incidents from their own experience in an audible voice.
You will need: Copies of *Tiddler.*

What to do

- Use the book to talk about the different personality types in the story. There are good talkers, listeners and storytellers; imaginative people and quiet people; leaders and followers.
- Explain to the class that in real life different circumstances bring out different aspects of peoples' personalities.
- Invite the children to think about a character from *Tiddler.* For example, ask: *Why does Tiddler dawdle and not go straight to school?* How many reasons can they suggest? Is he lazy, tired, seeking adventure, nosy, inquisitive, easily distracted, or maybe just wants to be noticed?
- Point out that Little Johnny Dory first says he 'likes' Tiddler's story and, later, he 'loves' Tiddler's story. Ask: *Is it Tiddler's gift of tall-story-telling that Little Johnny Dory admires most?*
- Encourage the children to consider someone they admire and what they like about them. invite them tell a partner a story that shows the qualities of this person.
- Bring the children together and ask the listeners to describe their friend's hero. Allow the speakers to correct or embellish these accounts.

Differentiation
For older learners: Challenge the children to tell the whole class a story about something they did with a good friend.
For younger learners: Ask the children open questions to find out why they chose their hero. Ask: *How do they make you feel happy? What was the best time you spent with them?*

Fooling with the fishes

Objective: To experiment with and build new stores of words to communicate in different contexts.
You will need: Copies of *Tiddler,* photocopiable page 23, writing materials, dictionaries.

What to do

- Invite the children to find out the names of sea creatures in *Tiddler.* They may need help spelling some of the illustrated creatures.
- Ask the children to list these on the photocopiable sheet, along with a verb beginning with the same letter, as in 'diving with a dolphin' on the first spread.
- Encourage the children to create a collection of new alliterative activities using exciting and descriptive verbs. Remind them that they should stretch their imaginations, just like Tiddler.
- See how long they can keep the rhythm going, without repeating a phrase.
- Play a variation of 'tag', in which one child is the teacher, Miss Skate, and another is the fisherman. The rest each choose a different fish name. Miss Skate calls out one of the names, and says 'Redfin, come to school!' That child tries to reach Miss Skate without being caught by the fisherman. Once all the children are either in the 'school' or in the 'net', those in the school can try to release the ones in the net by touching them, without being caught themselves.

Differentiation
For older/more confident learners: Encourage the children to sort their sea creatures and verbs alphabetically or transfer their list to computer to automatically sort. Offer challenging verbs for them to look up in a dictionary, such as 'eluding an eel'.
For younger/less confident learners: Provide the children with name and verb word cards for them to sort by the onset letter. Support them to put these into the sentence orally.

Tiddler's tips

Objective: To explain their views to others in a small group, and decide how to report the group's views to the class.
You will need: Copies of *Tiddler,* photocopiable page 24, writing materials.
Cross-curricular link: PSHE.

What to do

- Discuss how Tiddler's behaviour differs from his friends'. Ask: *Does Tiddler go to school with friends or alone? Does he tell anyone where he is going or what he is doing? Is he truthful?* What advice could Tiddler offer his friends based on his experiences (or imagination)? What could they learn from his adventures?
- List the children's suggestions under headings. For example: 'Do [go straight to school]'; 'Do not [swim inside a bottle]'; 'Beware of [sharks]'.
- In groups discuss what advice they could give to their friends about going to and from school, in school and after school. Invite each group to make notes on their photocopiable sheet.
- Encourage the groups to present their suggestions in an interesting way to the class. For example, they might take turns to recite each tip; use an interview format; plan a short drama; or write a song, using percussion for appropriate emphasis.
- Listen to each group's presentation and discuss the merits of each.

Differentiation
For older/more confident learners: Develop the best presentation into a performance for an assembly or to present to another class.
For younger/less confident learners: Help the children to write cue cards to increase their confidence during the presentation.

Missing!

Help to fill out this 'missing' poster for Tiddler, using words and pictures.

MISSING!

Have you seen Tiddler?

This is Tiddler.
(draw him)

Description: ______________________________

____

____

REWARD!

____

Last seen at ______________________________

by ______________________________

at ______________________________

If seen, report to ______________________________

Fooling with the fishes

Write down the names of some sea creatures and exciting verbs that start with the same letter, like the first two examples. Tell these to a partner.

Verb	Sea creature
diving	dolphin
sailing	seal

Tiddler's tips

Fill in the boxes below. Think about the following questions: How can you keep safe on your way to and from school? What about in school and after school?

Do...

- ________________________
- ________________________
- ________________________

Do not...

- ________________________
- ________________________
- ________________________

Beware of...

- ________________________
- ________________________
- ________________________

Make notes below on how to present your groups tips.

____

____

____

SCHOLASTIC
www.scholastic.co.uk

Get writing

SECTION 6

Tall stories

Objective: To sustain form in narrative, including use of person and time.
You will need: Copies of *Tiddler,* Extract 2 on photocopiable page 9, writing materials, thesauruses.

What to do

- Ask: *Do you believe Tiddler's stories partly, completely, or not at all? Which are easier or harder to believe? Why? Do tall stories have credible elements?*
- Display Extract 2 and highlight "Sorry I'm late". Underline the verbs as they are identified.
- Invite a child to describe their journey to school. Ask them to retell their story, but now add something untrue, such as 'We stopped at the zebra crossing, for a monkey to cross'. Prompt them to develop their story by asking questions such as 'What did the monkey do then?'. Encourage them to use descriptive verbs.
- Let the children relate their own made-up excuses to a partner. Encourage listeners to ask questions to help their partners' to stretch the truth to the limit.
- Ask the children to write down their tall stories, under the title 'Sorry I'm late'. They should write in the first person and the past tense.
- Remind the children to keep some aspects plausible. Explain that they should tell their story in prose narrative.

Differentiation
For older/more confident learners: Encourage the children to read their stories aloud, checking punctuation, consistency of person and tense and using the thesaurus to substitute exciting verbs.
For younger/less confident learners: Allow the children to work in pairs, sharing ideas. Have an adult act as scribe if necessary.

Character and setting

Objective: To use key features of narrative in their own writing
You will need: Copies of *Tiddler,* enlarged copies of photocopiable page 28, writing materials.

What to do

- Talk about the fact that all the characters in *Tiddler* are sea creatures. Ask: *Would it be sensible for Tiddler to meet an elephant or a mouse? Could he use the excuse "I was chased by a tarantula?" Why not?*
- Invite the children to use the plot of *Tiddler,* but change the characters and setting. For example, a worm called Squiggler has a big imagination. He makes excuses to his teacher, Miss Worm, such as "Sorry I'm late. I was dug up by a blackbird and fell from its beak in mid-flight."
- Remind the children that all the characters should be realistic within the setting. Squiggler could not meet a whale or a squid. Squiggler's teacher should not present a danger to him, such as a mole.
- Hand out copies of the photocopiable sheet to help the children to use as a storyboard to plan their own story. Keep copies of *Tiddler* handy for them to use as reference.
- Encourage the children to write in the past tense and third person, using speech marks for direct speech.

Differentiation
For older/more confident learners: Challenge the children to tell parts of their story in verse.
For younger/less confident learners: Help the children come up with a good ending for their tale.

The anatomy of a fish

Objective: To convey information and ideas in simple non-narrative forms.
You will need: Copies of *Tiddler,* writing materials, comprehensive dictionaries, scrap paper or chalk boards, photocopiable page 29.
Cross-curricular link: Science.

What to do

- Look at the little fish at school on the second spread of *Tiddler.* Explain that they are busy drawing fish skeletons on their slates.
- Invite the children to look at a drawing of a human skeleton.
- Discuss the bones we have in common with a fish, such as the skull and ribs. Point out that we do not usually see our skeletons as they are covered in flesh, but that they are part of our bodily structure.
- Hand out copies of the photocopiable sheet and invite the children to label the drawing, using the words from the box, and drawing the lines in the appropriate places with a ruler.
- When the children have completed labelling their fish diagram, ask them if there are any other parts of a fish that they know, such as the lateral line.

Differentiation
For older learners: Challenge the children to research further fishy facts, such as how fins help with movements (turning, speed, balance) and the purpose of the lateral line.
For younger learners: Write the names of the different parts of the fish on the board, and help the children to put them into alphabetical order.

Have you seen...?

Objective: To compose and write simple sentences independently to communicate meaning.
You will need: Enlarged copies of *Tiddler,* Extract 1 on photocopiable page 8, writing materials.

What to do

- Show the children an enlarged copy of Extract 1. Ask: *Which phrases describe Tiddler's appearance and which refer to his behaviour?*
- Ask them to imagine they were looking for Tiddler. Ask: *What information would help to describe Tiddler to other sea creatures?*
- Draw the children's attention to how we use the present tense when describing someone. Look at the use of the past tense in the extract. Explain that it is fine to use either tense when writing a story, but for a description, we write as we speak, in the present tense.
- Open the book at different spreads and invite the children to describe different characters, such as the lobster and eel. Encourage them to use their imaginations to embellish the descriptions. For example, 'the lobster clicks his front claws noisily'.
- Ask the children to complete the sentence: 'Have you seen...' with the character's name or species and a question mark. Invite them write two or three sentences describing the character, using details from the book.

Differentiation
For older/more confident learners: Invite the children to read their descriptions without the opening question. Ask the rest of the class to guess who the character is.
For younger/less confident learners: Prompt the children to consider characteristics such as colour, size, shape, habits and sounds.

Get writing

SECTION 6

Rhyme time

Objective: To develop an understanding of phonics and poetry as a narrative form.
You will need: Copies of *Tiddler,* Extract 3 on photocopiable page 10, whiteboard or flipchart, writing materials.

What to do

- Read Extract 3 together and explain that, although it is rhyming verse, the words form sentences as in story narrative.
- Demonstrate the different layout by rewriting the words as sentences. Do the children spot the differences, such as line length, layout and the upper case 'd' in 'dreaming'?
- Explain to the class that *Tiddler* is a rhyming story. As a class, have a go at making up some more fishy rhymes. Start by choosing a fish or sea creature with a name, that has one syllable, such as a skate, sole or whale. Ask the children to think of rhyming words and write these on the whiteboard.
- Next, see if these suggestions give you any ideas for a class poem, for example 'Limp shrimp' or the 'Odd cod'.
- Cut out the words from the photocopiable and match them into rhyming pairs. Explain that they don't have to be spelt the same to rhyme. Using the book, can the children find other examples of words that rhyme?

Differentiation
For older/more confident learners: Challenge the children to write their own poem, experimenting with pictures and layout.
For younger/less confident learners: Cover up the last words in each line of the extract, and see if the children can guess what they are. Allow children to work in pairs to make up their own poem, using words from the sheet (with adult help if required).

Eyewitness

Objective: To use key features of narrative in their own writing.
You will need: Copies of *Tiddler,* Extract 2 on photocopiable page 9, writing materials.
Cross curricular link: Drama

What to do

- Invite individual children to read out the direct speech from Extract 2. Ask: *What do the capital letters convey? Why is Tiddler shouting?* (The answer is to convince his friends and his teacher.) *Who could back up his story if it were true? Who was there at the time and saw everything?*
- Explain that the mermaid, if she exists, is an eyewitness because she saw everything.
- Ask the children to list any eyewitnesses who could support Tiddler's stories. Make sure they include those who are not mentioned in the text but appear in the illustrations.
- Ask the children to find a partner and pretend to be one of Tiddler's eyewitnesses. Their partner should question them about what they saw. What time was it? What were they doing? Why did they notice Tiddler?
- Let partners swap roles after five minutes and have copies of *Tiddler* handy for reference.
- Ask the children to write up their eyewitness account. Remind them to include phrases that show the passage of time, such as 'at ten o'clock' and 'meanwhile'.

Differentiation
For older/more confident learners: Invite other children to comment on how convincing their narratives are.
For younger/more confident learners: Allow the children to tell their stories with an adult acting as scribe. Encourage them to read back what they said and copy it in their own handwriting.

Character and setting

Plan a story based on *Tiddler,* but with different characters and setting.

Story title: ______________________________

My new character's name was	He/she was a	He/she lived
One day, he/she had a scary adventure. This is what happened...	He/she was frightened because	He/she escaped! This is how:

The end.

The anatomy of a fish

Label the drawing using the words from the box.

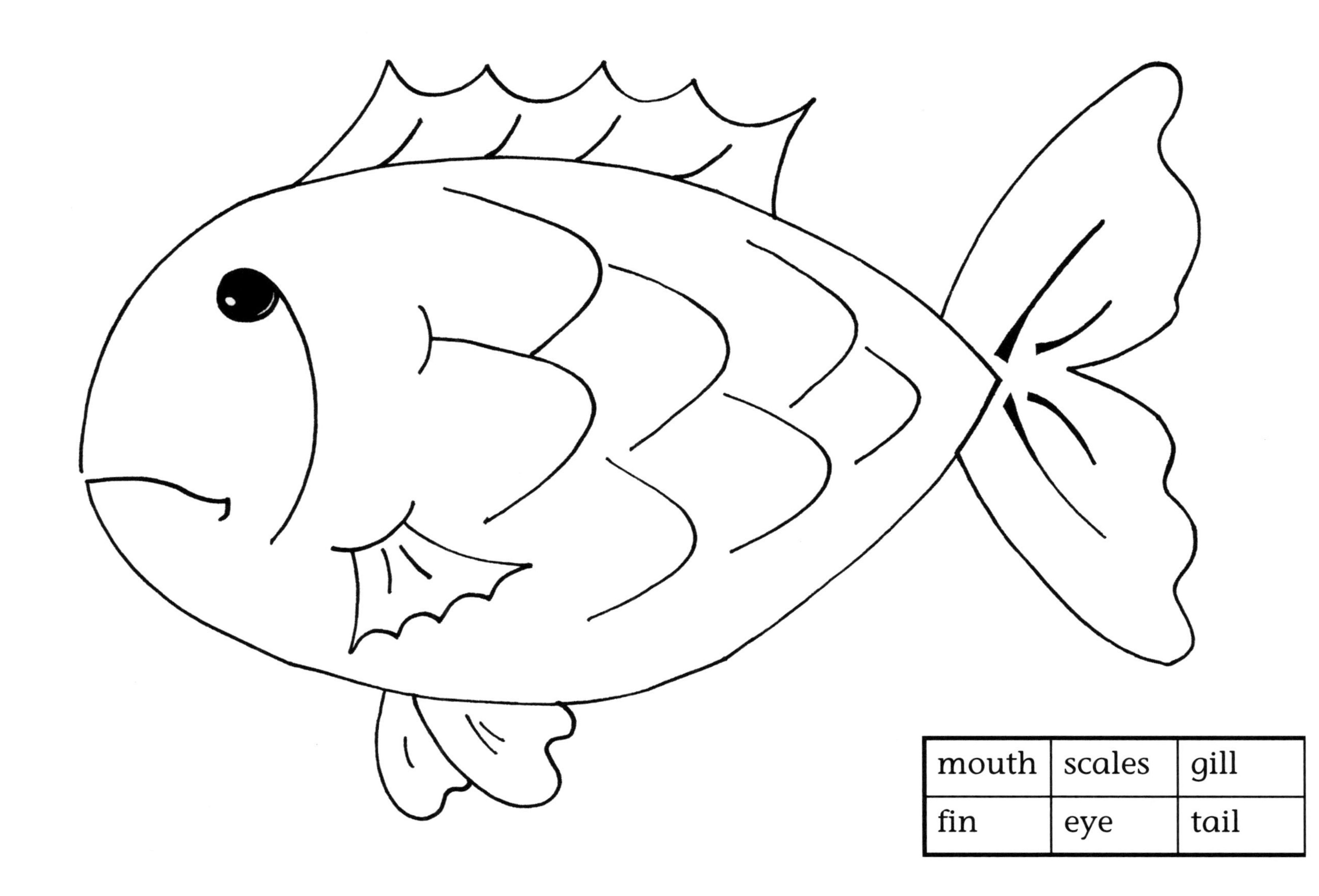

mouth	scales	gill
fin	eye	tail

Rhyme time

Cut out the words and match them in rhyming pairs.

seal	**tail**
plaice	**bubble**
eel	**dace**
whale	**trouble**

www.scholastic.co.uk

Assessment

SECTION 7

Assessment advice

The children will immediately warm to the character of Tiddler, enjoying his naughtiness vicariously. The undersea setting is distant enough for the children to feel safe, while being able to empathise with the familiar situations: going to school, being late, being tempted to dawdle and inventing excuses.

Make the most of children's discussion about the different viewpoints, from Tiddler through to his teacher and the chain of storytellers. Look for relevance and explanation in their individual responses.

The lyrical swing of the rhyming verse invites the children to join in and makes the story as memorable as it is enjoyable. Pausing before rhyming words and repeated phrases will indicate how aware the children are of the patterned language. In reading aloud, the rhymes and repetition will also increase their confidence. Look out for readers comparing rhyming words as they decode them.

Every spread offers scope for descriptive and analytical dialogue: Ask:

- *How much storyline is carried in the pictures rather than the text?*
- *Which parts of each picture directly illustrate the words?*
- *Where has the illustrator used his imagination to interpret the author's words?*
- *How might the children interpret the words if they were the illustrators?*

Encourage the children to read and re-read the book individually and in small groups. Invite them to read aloud with more than one expressive voice and emphasising the pantomime repetition of Tiddler's claims' being refuted and endorsed.

Fishing for answers

Assessment focus: To identify the main events and characters in stories, and find specific information in simple texts.
What you need: Copies of *Tiddler*, photocopiable page 32, writing materials.

What to do

- After the children have read and re-read the book, ask them what they thought of it. Ask: *Did you think it was fun? Did you enjoy it? Would you read it again? Is it a memorable story? Which characters do you like best?*
- Hand out copies of the photocopiable sheet. Tell the children to read each question carefully before writing their answer. Allow them access to *Tiddler* to check any answers they are unsure of.
- Be aware that the questions form part of the assessment, testing the children's comprehension and passive vocabulary. The children will need to understand and apply the meanings of words, such as 'apology' and 'mythical', in order to answer these questions (although clues are given in the structure of the question). Younger children may need these terms explained.
- Talk about other books by Julia Donaldson, illustrated by Axel Scheffler, to help the children recognise the toothy Gruffalo fish chasing poor Tiddler around in circles.
- Explain that the last question has no definitive answer. They should answer with their own opinions and explain why. They may need to write on the back of their page or on a separate sheet of paper. When marking this, look for justification of their choice of character and the part they play in the story. Look for signs that they appreciate the character's nature and purpose in the story.

Fishing for answers

Answer these questions about the book *Tiddler.*

1. Ring the correct definition of a 'tall tale':

a long story **a made-up story** **a story for children**

2. What words of apology does Tiddler use every day when he arrives late?

____

____

3. Which mythical character in the story is not a real sea creature?

____

4. Who believes all Tiddler's stories?

____

5. Why is the word 'NET' in capital letters?

____

____

6. When Tiddler tracks his story back home, who is the first character to recognise him?

____

7. If you could be one character in the story, who would it be and why?

____

____

____

____